Geckos for Beginners

Basics of Species Appropriate Husbandry and Care in Your Terrarium

ALINA DARIA

ISBN: 9798533822435

Contents

Introduction

The gecko family, whose scientific name is *Gekkonidae*, belongs to the order *Squamata* and the superorder *Lepidosauria.* Geckos are reptiles. The primary home of most geckos is in tropical areas, but some species are also found in very dry and rocky areas. Since the gecko family has been around for many millions of years - about fifty million years to be exact! – these animals have spread over a large area of the world and adapted well to the conditions in different areas.

The family includes 55 genera and even more than one thousand different gecko species! Many species have probably not even been discovered yet. The species and genera sometimes differ considerably and - depending on the area of distribution - have sometimes evolved quite differently.

Not all of the more than a thousand species are kept as pets. In the domestic terrarium, for example, the leopard gecko genus, the day gecko genus, the crested gecko species or the tokay species are quite common.

Geckos are so different that their size also varies depending on the genus / species - in fact, the smallest geckos measure only about two centimetres (*0.8 inches*). The largest species grow to about forty centimetres long (*15 inches*). Some species, which are now already extinct, became even larger - the extinct Kawekaweau gecko could reach a size of about sixty centimetres (*23 inches*)!

Not all geckos are nocturnal, but the majority of them are. About three out of four gecko species are nocturnal - or at least crepuscular. These species are usually plain and inconspicuous in colour, so they do not attract too much attention. Furthermore, their eyes are adapted to living primarily in the dark, as they have slit pupils.

In addition, the toes of the different species also differ. In this respect, geckos can be divided into the so-called clawed geckos and lamellar geckos.

Lamellar geckos have an extremely high power of adhesion, thanks to which they can run up steep walls - and they can even walk upside down on ceilings! But how is this possible? Lamellar geckos owe this ability to their special feet, which are covered with many billions of hairs. Through these fine hairs, they make use of electrostatic forces and the interaction between molecules and atoms, which enables them to walk on ceilings and walls.

The clawed geckos, on the other hand, are unable to do this.

Geckos are cold-blooded animals - this characteristic applies to all reptiles. An alternately warm animal adjusts its body temperature to the ambient temperature.

© *Anrita*

Popular Pet Geckos

There are currently about 1,200 discovered gecko species, which can be divided into more than fifty genera. However, not all gecko genera or species are well suited for the home terrarium. In the meantime, some geckos have emerged as ideal pets whose needs can also be met at home in a species-appropriate way. Therefore, we would like to take a closer look at some of the most popular geckos in the following!

1. Leopard geckos

The leopard gecko, whose scientific name is "*Eublepharis macularius*", is the most commonly kept pet of all geckos in terrariums and is considered a beginner-friendly reptile. However, good preparation is the be-all and end-all for any animal husbandry - this applies as well to the beginner-friendly leopard gecko. Leopard geckos belong to the subfamily of eyelid geckos, whose scientific name is "*Eublepharidae*". Eyelid geckos, unlike other geckos, have eyelids and are usually ground dwellers; they are not as good climbers as other geckos because they do not have adhesive lamellae on their feet. Leopard geckos reach a body size of about 25 to 30 centimetres (*10 to 12 inches*) and are nocturnal / crepuscular. Leopard geckos can reach an age of about 30 years and some animals have been known to live even longer. However, the average lifespan of the leopard gecko is closer to about 15 years.

Leopard gecko – © Sandra Frank

2. Day geckos

Day geckos are a genus of geckos whose species are generally diurnal. This distinguishes them from many other geckos, as the majority of geckos tend to be nocturnal. The scientific name of this genus is "*Phelsuma*", so day geckos are also called phelsuma. Day geckos are very colourful animals that are often green or yellow and often have patterns (for example red spots). Day geckos are usually somewhat smaller than leopard geckos; their size can range from 8 to 30 centimetres (*3 to 12 inches*), depending on the species. In the wild, they are mainly found in Madagascar, but also on other islands in the Indian Ocean. The average lifespan is about eight to ten years.

Madagascar day gecko – © Photo Rabe

3. Tokay geckos

Tokays are nocturnal / crepuscular geckos that are quite large. They can reach a body length of about 35 centimetres (*14 inches*). They are also quite colourful, but usually do not shine in quite as bright colours as day geckos. The colourations of the tokay are usually somewhat plainer, for example grey-blue or grey-brown. They also usually have patterns on their bodies; blue and/or red spots are common. Tokays are native to Asian countries such as Bangladesh, India, Taiwan and also southern China.

Tokay gecko – © Josch13

4. Crested geckos

Crested geckos are a species of geckos that belongs to the genus *Correlophus*. Crested geckos also belong to the double-fingered gecko family, whose scientific name is *Diplodactylidae*. They were long thought to be extinct but were fortunately rediscovered in the 1990s. Their range is not large, as they are generally only found on the islands of Ile des Pins and Grande Terre. These belong to the archipelago of New Caledonia in the southern Pacific Ocean. Crested geckos live in the wild mainly on and in trees. Thanks to the adhesive lamellae on their feet, crested geckos are excellent climbers and have no problems living in trees. Crested geckos also belong to the nocturnal geckos, but they are not as colourful as the previously mentioned geckos. The colours of Crested geckos are rather plain and usually quite inconspicuous (brown, grey, plain green, pale yellow, pale red). Crested geckos can also live for more than twenty years if kept in a species-appropriate manner at home.

Crested gecko

5. Moorish wall geckos

Moorish wall geckos, whose scientific name is "*Tarentola mauritanica*", belong to the genus Tarentola. They are so-called leaf finger geckos. Moorish wall geckos are native to large parts of the Mediterranean region, for example Spain, Portugal, Italy, Croatia and France. But Moorish wall geckos are also often found in North African countries such as Egypt. They grow to about 15 to 16 centimetres (*6 inches*) and are quite inconspicuous. Their colouring is very plain and includes calm earth tones like brown, beige or even black. Moorish wall geckos, like the majority of geckos, are also nocturnal or crepuscular animals. Like crested geckos, Moorish wall geckos have adhesive lamellae under their feet, which makes them exceptionally good climbers - even on very slippery surfaces. However, Moorish wall geckos do not live in trees, but instead mostly under rocks or hidden between walls.

Moorish wall gecko – © Ulrike Leone

6. Short-fingered geckos

The scientific name of short-fingered geckos is *Stenodactylus sthenodactylus*. They belong to the very small geckos because they only grow to about 10 centimetres (*4 inches*). Their life expectancy is also quite a bit shorter, as short-fingered geckos live for about five years on average. But even though these geckos are so small, they are very noisy. In dangerous situations or when they feel unwell, they make very shrill and loud whistling noises. Short-fingered geckos are also nocturnal.

7. Algerian sand geckos

Algerian sand geckos (*Tropiocolotes steudneri*) belong to the very small geckos as well. Due to their size, these small geckos are also referred to collectively as *dwarf geckos*. Algerian sand geckos are found in scree deserts and sandy deserts, mainly in African countries such as Morocco, Egypt or Tunisia. Algerian sand geckos grow to only 5 to 7 centimetres (*2 to 3 inches*) in size and are thus definitely among the smallest geckos. Their colours are very plain and reminiscent of their home in the African deserts - light yellow, light or dark beige, sometimes a stronger yellow. In addition, their small body is covered with a dotted pattern, which is usually brown or white. Algerian sand geckos are also among the nocturnal geckos.

Group and Socialisation

The different gecko genera or gecko species are also sometimes quite different in terms of their social behaviour. In the wild, many geckos live together in so-called "loose associations".

However, there are also many gecko species that are strict loners and actually only visit another gecko during mating season. At this time, the males are quite aggressive and sometimes even bite into the neck of the chosen female. The female, on the other hand, can "store" the sperm of the male gecko in her body for quite a long time and still lay fertilised eggs after mating.

The ever-popular leopard geckos are best kept alone, as they are solitary animals in the wild anyway. Sometimes leopard geckos do spend time together in the wild, but this is not the rule and they do not consciously seek contact with each other; unless they want to breed.

Nevertheless, keeping leopard geckos in groups rather than singly is also possible. However, care should be taken that two male leopard geckos never have to live together, because this species is very dominant and usually does not tolerate any intruder in its territory. Therefore, sooner or later two males will most likely fight, injure and in the worst case even kill each other. If you want to keep leopard geckos in a harem, the male should enjoy the company of at least three females - because the dominant leopard gecko would probably stress even two females too much.

In any case, these females should already be fully grown. But you never have a guarantee that keeping a group will work in the long run. Females also only tolerate each other and sometimes attack each other, even if they have lived together peacefully for years!

Especially for beginners, however, it is better to "play it safe" and keep a leopard gecko (whether male or female) alone. In female-only groups, there is less danger of the animals quarrelling and fighting, but females also have their individual characters, which do not always fit together. Females usually tolerate each other, but the danger of a fight always exists. Even after many years. Therefore, keeping them singly is recommended.

Keeping a male alone is even more suitable for a beginner than keeping a female alone. Both types of keeping are easier than group keeping, but there are a few more points to consider when keeping a female.

During the mating season, females often take breaks from feeding, regardless of whether they have a partner or not. You have to be prepared for this.

Keeping a female alone can also lead to so-called "egg binding". This can occur not only in reptiles like the gecko, but also in amphibians, birds and fish. It can happen that eggs are formed, but these cause a "blockage" and are not laid.

The reason for this is often that there is no male to animate and fertilise the eggs. Sometimes the eggs are also deformed. The cloaca may also prolapse as a result of egg binding. Although this tends to occur rather rarely, it is a risk factor that is not present when keeping a male.

However, if you want to keep geckos in a group, you should always make sure that the animals have even more space available than if they are kept individually. The terrarium must offer enough space so that the animals can get out of each other's way whenever they wish. Also, enough hiding places are necessary so that a gecko can always retreat when it needs its rest.

The situation is similar with day geckos. Day geckos may be kept in pairs, which can be problem-free if the geckos get along well. However, even after several months or years, it can still happen that the geckos quarrel and living together is no longer possible. Therefore, it is necessary to switch to two separate terrariums in such a case.

In principle, however, there is nothing to be said against keeping a day gecko alone, although some keepers have reported in the past that their day geckos became somewhat lazy when kept alone. Whether this is due to a lack of a companion cannot be clearly stated at this time.

Day geckos are also very dominant, so keeping them in pairs with two males is not advisable. A male day gecko will not accept another male in his territory and in all likelihood, there will be power struggles. Day geckos belong to the more aggressive gecko species. Therefore, the advantages of keeping them individually outweigh the disadvantages.

Tokay geckos are considered the "louder" of the geckos. The tokay gecko is nocturnal and likes to call for a female during mating season if it lives in solitary confinement. If it has conspecifics - or if one or two female tokays are kept - the problem of loud calls does not usually occur. The mating calls of a male tokay gecko can actually be very loud - sometimes as loud as the barking of a dog. And this is not very pleasant, especially at night time.

Tokay – © Shark Lin

The crested gecko is similar to the leopard gecko, day gecko and tokay gecko in this respect. It is also a solitary animal, so keeping a male alone is also a good idea if you want to avoid the risk of egg binding. A male crested gecko should not live with other males either, as he also becomes quite aggressive when defending his territory. If you are more experienced in keeping them, you can try an all-female group or a harem. However, there is never a guarantee that living together will be successful! Too much depends on the individual character traits of the geckos.

However, if you decide against keeping them individually and opt for a harem, you will inevitably have to ask yourself what to do with the fertilised eggs. In principle, breeding belongs in the hands of very experienced gecko keepers who have several years of experience to show. A layperson and beginners should not breed as a matter of principle. Successful breeding requires background knowledge - also regarding genetics - and a lot of responsibility must be taken.

Neutering is neither sensible nor possible with geckos. Therefore, in mixed groups, mating will inevitably occur.

One option is to let the eggs hatch and not take the young out of the terrarium after they hatch. Most gecko species have no family ties and will sooner or later regard the little gecko babies as food and eat them. This sounds barbaric, but it is quite common among reptiles and amphibians. For example, axolotls, which are amphibians, do not develop deep friendships or a parent-child relationship. They often do not identify their own children and confuse them with small fish that serve as food. The same often happens with geckos and other reptile and amphibian species.

Whether one can live with it is an ethical question. Many people cannot and do not want to. Therefore, many keepers choose to take the fertilised eggs out of the terrarium after egg laying and freeze them. After freezing, the eggs are disposed of. If you decide to use this method, the eggs must not be disposed of immediately. Freezing is essential to prevent a small gecko from developing in the egg if it has already been discarded.

If you do not consider both options and cannot ethically reconcile them, it is best to keep only one female or one male in solitary husbandry. Keeping them singly is the safest form of husbandry anyway, and also the least stressful for the gecko. Furthermore, keeping them individually prevents fights, which can happen suddenly at any time - even if geckos have been living peacefully together for years.

So far, so good. But can geckos be socialised with other animal species? The simple answer is: No. On the one hand, other animal species have completely different habitat requirements. On the other hand, they cannot communicate with each other properly. Often there are fights, one animal sees the other animal as prey, etc.

In the past, some keepers had the idea of socialising geckos with bearded dragons, for example. This is not recommended at all, as the two species require different living conditions, which cannot be achieved at the same time anyway. If you want to keep both reptiles, you will need two or more terrariums.

Genders

Gender identification can be quite difficult with geckos. In general, it is not only with geckos that it is usually somewhat more complicated to determine the gender, but also with many other reptiles and amphibians.

With young animals, gender determination is often impossible and can only be realised when the animal gets older. In some cases, the gender can only be reliably identified from the age of two to three months. In other species, this is only possible after half a year or after one year. This always depends on the gecko species. Breeders of certain species are sometimes able to determine the gender with certainty after one month, even though errors cannot usually be completely ruled out.

Therefore, the gender determination should be left to an experienced breeder or gecko expert for the respective species. Unfortunately, mistakes are often made in pet shops, too, and geckos of the wrong gender are given away, as the staff in pet shops are usually not experts for geckos.

Males usually have two hemipenis pockets and preanal pores. These are very pronounced. The females mostly also have preanal pores, but they are less pronounced than those of the males.

The term "hemi" comes from ancient Greek and means "half". The term "hemipenis" therefore means something like "half penis". The term is used to describe the male genital organ or mating organ of the squamata - i.e., also the organ of a male gecko. They are located at the side of the cloaca within an expandable pouch. Sometimes they are also located below the cloaca, often at the base of the tail. The hemipenis pouches with the hemipenis form quite early, whereas the preanal pores usually develop later, when a gecko becomes pubescent. The preanal pores are located above the cloaca and form a kind of triangle in many species.

The females of many gecko species (e.g., day geckos or crested geckos) also form “calcium sacs” behind the head on the neck. These are especially visible before egg-laying. In these sacs the female stores calcium, which is needed for the formation of the eggs.

The cloacal area of females is in most cases flatter than the cloacal area of males, as females usually do not have hemipenis pockets. Occasionally, however, a female may also have a poorly developed pocket in this area. The preanal pores of a female may also be more pronounced than usual. This is another reason why gender determination is often quite difficult - especially for a layperson.

In most gecko species, the males have a stronger and broader head than the females, and the females usually remain smaller than the males. These can be further clues to the gender, although there can of course be differences here - as in humans. In order to be able to clearly identify the gender, the genital organs must be looked at in any case.

Baby gecko – © Roland Steinmann

Purchasing Geckos

If one wants to acquire pets, many people almost automatically turn to a conventional pet shop. However, pet shops unfortunately often give the wrong advice, as the staff are often not specially trained in reptile care. This is not only the case with reptiles such as geckos, but also with other popular pets such as rodents, amphibians, fish, etc. Therefore, it is advisable to at least take the information from pet shops with a grain of salt.

Furthermore, pet shops often sell animals that are not ready to be given away - some animals are injured, some animals are sick, some animals are still too young. It will usually be difficult for a layperson to judge whether an animal is ready to be given away.

It is therefore more advisable to buy reptiles such as geckos from a reputable breeder. Reputable breeders either concentrate on one specific species of gecko or on only a few different species. This allows them to gain a lot of experience and they are experts in their respective field. At the time of take-over, the animals must be healthy, must not show any injuries and must be old enough. It is not necessary for a gecko to be fully grown when it is surrendered, but it must at least have reached its appropriate weight.

A reputable breeder will pay attention to all these points and give the new owner comprehensive advice. Serious breeders attach great importance to the fact that their animals come to nice and species-appropriate homes and are therefore also happy to answer any remaining questions. The animal will also be prepared for transport.

Of course, it is also an option to adopt a gecko from a reptile care centre, animal shelter or get it second-hand. Care centres and animal shelters can usually provide proper advice as well. Taking a gecko second-hand because it is no longer wanted in its old home is also a commendable decision. However, there is a risk of unintentionally taking on a sick animal that would be better off in expert hands until it is healthy again.

Leopard gecko Eublepharis – © Markéta Machová

The Terrarium

At your home, geckos are kept in a terrarium. And they need space! There are no legally binding regulations regarding the minimum size of the terrarium, but in the gecko community quite sensible minimum dimensions have become established in the meantime, based on experience with the reptiles.

An absolute minimum size is generally considered to be a terrarium length of 80 centimetres (*30 inches*), a width of 40 centimetres (*16 inches*) and a height of 40 centimetres (*16 inches*). These dimensions should not be undercut under any circumstances, as otherwise the gecko would have to live in far too confined a space.

However, the dimensions 100 x 50 x 50 centimetres (*40 x 20 x 20 inches*) are often recommended as minimum dimensions. This is generally more acceptable, as a gecko should have half a square metre of floor space at its disposal. In general, the larger the better!

These dimensions apply to a gecko kept individually. If you dare to keep a group (see chapter "Group and Socialisation"), you should add about 20 centimetres (*8 inches*) in length per additional animal. A somewhat larger terrarium should also be chosen in width and height.

These measurements may differ from what has been read or heard so far. On 10 January 1997, the Federal Ministry of Food and Agriculture published a report by the expert group on the minimum requirements for keeping reptiles. This states the basic formula "4 x 3 x 2". This formula is multiplied by the so-called HTL (head-torso length) of the gecko.

For example, if you have a gecko with a HTL of 15 centimetres (*6 inches*), the minimum dimensions for the terrarium would be 60 centimetres long (*24 inches*), 45 centimetres wide (*18 inches*) and 30 centimetres high (*12 inches*).

This may have been fine almost 25 years ago in 1997 and appropriate to the state of knowledge at the time, but today it is common knowledge that geckos need more space.

Once the perfect terrarium has been found (or built), the question arises as to where it should find its place. In any case, it should not be exposed to direct sunlight, as otherwise the terrarium can heat up very strongly - if this is not noticed early on, an overheated terrarium can even lead to the death of the animal in the worst case. Ideally, the terrarium should not be placed directly next to a heater, as it is easier to control the temperature of the terrarium if there is no heater directly influencing it.

The terrarium should not be placed on the floor, but slightly elevated. This reduces the coldness on the ground and sometimes also draughts, and the gecko can be observed better if the terrarium is placed on a stable cabinet. All kinds of base cabinets that can withstand the weight of the terrarium are suitable, but also a stone base, as is often used for particularly heavy aquariums. Of course, you can also use your own constructions that can withstand the weight permanently.

Since most gecko species are nocturnal, a quiet place in the flat or house should be chosen. Too loud noises from a music system, TV or similar can disturb the gecko while it is sleeping - and are also not very nice when the gecko is awake. Of course, it doesn't have to be completely quiet; geckos also get used to a background of noise and to the sounds that are normally heard in their home. Nevertheless, these noises should not be so loud that the gecko becomes frightened, scared and possibly even shy.

In addition, a good air exchange should be ensured in the terrarium. Many terrariums already have a ventilation included. To ensure that the air exchange works well, and the air does not accumulate, the vents should be placed on two opposite sides. The vents should not be so large that the insects to be fed can escape through them. Therefore, attention should be paid to the size of the individual slits in the vents. There should be at least three vents per terrarium side so that the air can circulate well and does not stand still.

The topic of "substrate in the terrarium" is one of the most frequently debated topics in the gecko community. Opinions differ on this, and heated discussions regularly arise. For many amphibian and fish species, the issue of substrate is similar to that of reptiles such as geckos. Accepted standards also differ from country to country.

Most gecko breeders and keepers are of the opinion that loose sand should be avoided. This applies to all sand species. Sand as the sole substrate is not suitable for geckos. In general, loose substrate should be avoided.

However, it is possible to mix sand with clay. However, it is important to ensure that the proportion of sand is not too high, otherwise the mixture will not be hard enough as a substrate.

© *Torsten Simon*

A sand/clay mixture can either be bought or mixed yourself. For example, terrarium sand or fine play sand are suitable; fine building sand or bird sand also work. The sand is then mixed with clay powder, usually using about four parts sand to one part clay. The higher the proportion of clay, the harder the mixture will be.

The dry mixture is then mixed with water and needs some time to dry. Depending on the weather, this usually takes a few days. Finally, the substrate should no longer be too loose, but rather firm and rather hard.

A nice, firm loamy soil usually comes closest to the soil in the wild.

Another option for the substrate is cork boards. Cork boards are heat-insulating, which in turn will save energy. In addition, cork boards can be vacuumed quite easily and are also otherwise very easy to clean. Black cork in particular can also be used well in rainforest terrariums, as the cork both absorbs moisture and releases it back to the outside environment - so there is no danger of anything moulding in the terrarium due to too much moisture.

So-called quarry stone mosaic floors are also quite popular in gecko terrariums these days. For thermal insulation, most keepers and breeders first decide to cover the floor with a two to three centimetre (*1 inch*) thick Styrodur board. The quarry stone mosaic panels are then laid on top of this. Since the surface of the Styrodur sheets is quite rough, the mosaic tiles adhere very well to it. Quarry stone mosaic panels are available in different colours and thus bring a little more colour into the terrarium. To glue the quarry stone mosaic panels to the Styrodur panel, conventional tile glue is sufficient.

Another important aspect in the gecko terrarium is lighting or heat. Although most gecko species are predominantly nocturnal, they still need sufficient warmth and lighting during the day. Geckos regulate their body temperature with the help of their environment; unlike mammals, for example. Many reptiles, including geckos, therefore depend on external influences to regulate their body temperature.

In the terrarium, the gecko should have different heat zones available so that it can switch between them. The average temperature in the terrarium should be between about 25°C and 30°C. In addition, however, there should be a cooling area, where the temperature is approximately between 21°C and 25°C. A heating area is also necessary, where the temperature is about 35°C to 40°C.

To achieve this, a single spotlight placed either on the left or right is sufficient for most terrariums. The heating point should not be in the middle of the terrarium, but on one of the sides, so that the opposite side can be the cooling area. If the terrarium is particularly large, it may be necessary to fit two spot heaters shining on the same side. It is best to first test whether one spotlight is sufficient and measure the temperature in the three areas (left, centre, right).

If the gecko is not in brumation, the spotlight should be switched on for about 12 hours a day. During brumation, this is not necessary or even a hindrance, as the gecko's body is brought down to brumation mode by the gradually cooler temperatures.

The spotlight should not be a metal halide lamp, infrared light and UVB/UVC lighting are also rather unsuitable. Infrared lamps and UV radiation can cause injury and damage both the eyes and skin of the gecko. Burns to the gecko's skin and/or eyes are quite common with such lamps.

UV light does contribute to the formation of the important vitamin D3 - which is actually a hormone - but there is also a risk of injury. At the very least, great care should be taken when using it. Halogen lamps without LEDs and with reflector inserts are better suited. A night light, on the other hand, is not necessary. It is sufficient if the shutters of the windows are not completely closed and thus some moonlight shines in.

Geckos are used to darkness and need it for their day-night rhythm. Otherwise, they can get confused.

It is also important that a gecko has some hiding places available. Many geckos only come to rest completely in their hiding place, where they feel safe. The gecko should fit comfortably into the hiding place, but it should also not be too large. Ideal hiding places are those that are adapted to the body size of the gecko and are slightly larger than the animal itself. If the hiding place is too big, the gecko may not feel protected enough.

There are many possible hiding places. You can use caves made of bark or cork, halved flowerpots, cork oak bark, stone structures or roots. The so-called "wet boxes" are also very popular. These are burrows that are lined with damp moss. Sometimes they are also lined with moist coconut fibre humus. The humidity in the wetboxes is very high. However, in addition to at least one wet box, several dry hiding places should also be offered.

If you keep not only one but several geckos, each gecko should have at least one hiding place. It is better if one or two more hiding places are offered so that there is a choice.

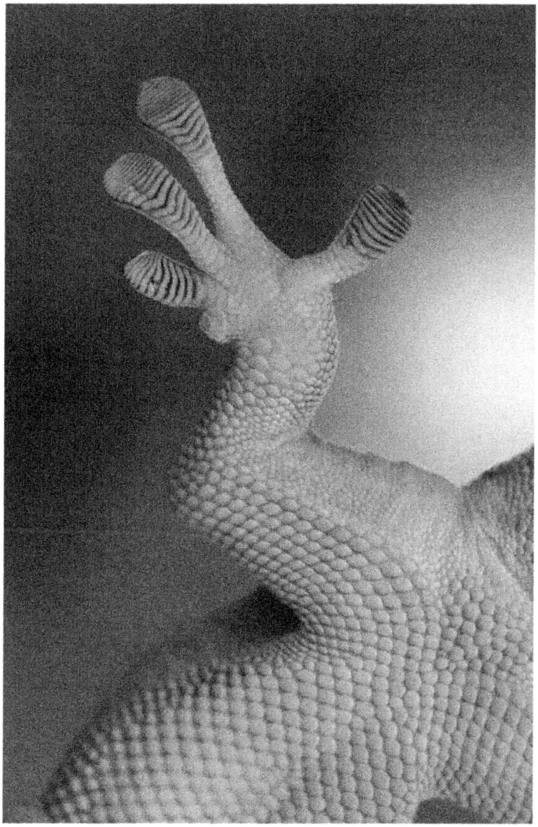

© *Rudy und Peter Skitterians*

In the hiding places, the gecko comes to rest, but when it is awake, it needs something to do besides eating. Many gecko species like to climb, and some species are really excellent climbers. Therefore, a gecko should not only be offered opportunities to hide, but also to climb.

Rough and thick branches are very suitable for climbing. These should be sturdily attached so that they cannot topple over or otherwise move too much. This could injure the gecko. A structured back wall with plateaus should also be present in the terrarium.

Ideally, the terrarium should also have at least two plants. Three to four plants are better and also look nicer. Plants also contribute to the correct climate and adequate humidity in the terrarium. Especially bow hemp and tillandsias are very suitable for planting in a gecko terrarium. Ground cover such as ivy and plants for the back wall such as Ficus pumila also fit well in the terrarium.

Diet and Nutrition

Animals are roughly divided into carnivores (meat eaters), herbivores (plant eaters), frugivores (fruit eaters) and omnivores ("everything" eaters). These head categories are often further subdivided into subcategories; for example, insectivores (insect eaters) belong to the carnivores - and leaf-eaters belong to the herbivores.

Not all geckos have the same diet, but the majority of gecko species are classified as almost pure insectivores. Most geckos feed mainly or exclusively on insects such as grasshoppers, crickets, flies and the like. Larger gecko species sometimes even eat smaller mammals such as small mice in the wild. In addition, there are many geckos that occasionally eat plant food such as fruits.

The gecko species that are mainly kept in domestic terrariums belong to the insectivores. The leopard gecko enjoys live food such as crickets, grasshoppers and cockroaches. The same applies to the day gecko and the tokay gecko, although the day gecko in particular also likes to eat a few fruits. The crested gecko also likes to eat fruit; so often, in fact, that it is usually classified as an omnivore rather than an insectivore. The crested gecko also uses mainly insects as the basis of its diet, but often eats overripe fruits as well.

In the wild, the gecko is responsible for finding its own food. It is a skilful hunter and moves around more in the wild than in the terrarium at home. Moreover, at home, the food is handed to it by its owner - therefore domesticated geckos are not used to managing their food intake on their own.

For this reason, it is the owner's responsibility to select and ration species-appropriate food. It is often observed that domesticated geckos hardly develop a feeling of satiety and eat more food than they need - if it is offered to them by a human. Therefore, humans must take care that the gecko neither becomes too thin nor too fat. Obesity is generally quite common in pets and there are also obese geckos in some cases. Geckos gain weight quite quickly, which can lead to various diseases in the long run. In this respect, animals are no different from humans, as many diseases in humans are also triggered or promoted by obesity. Excess weight and obesity are one of the most common causes of death in geckos.

The most popular and healthiest insects for geckos:

- Crickets (e.g., steppe crickets, short-winged crickets or Mediterranean crickets)
- Grasshoppers (e.g., migratory grasshoppers, desert grasshoppers)
- Mealworms (sparingly; many calories!)
- Cockroaches (e.g., Argentine cockroaches)
- Flies
- Spiders

Insects can be fed alive or dead. However, there are countries where live feeding - even of insects - is not permitted by law. Sometimes live feeding is not prohibited in principle, but is handled much more strictly when vertebrates are fed than when invertebrates are fed.

The interests of the hunter are opposed to the interests of the prey animal. On the one hand, some animal species, such as the gecko, are naturally hunters and have a hunting instinct that they should be able to act out. On the other hand, prey animals also have rights, and, in principle, no harm may be done to them without good reason. Prey animals, for example, may feel extreme fear and suffer from not being able to flee from the hunter. For example, in many countries it is now forbidden to feed live mice to snakes. There are sometimes only a few exceptions to this ban.

In most countries, the requirements for feeding live insects are not as strict, as insects are invertebrates. Feeding geckos, for example, is therefore allowed, but the prey animals must also be cared for appropriately and must not suffer unnecessarily or be mistreated.

Whether to feed live insects is therefore also an ethical question. Most gecko keepers feed their insects in live form, as this allows geckos to live out their hunting instinct and is most similar to what they would eat in the wild. Most gecko species are not scavengers; scavengers feed on animals that are already dead and do not kill them themselves. There are geckos that will not touch dead insects.

To simulate that a dead insect is still alive, there are so-called "vibrating feeding stations". In many cases, however, these do not fulfil their purpose, as most geckos can tell whether the insect is still alive or already dead.

Furthermore, living insects contain important nutrients for the gecko, which are often lost with dead insects.

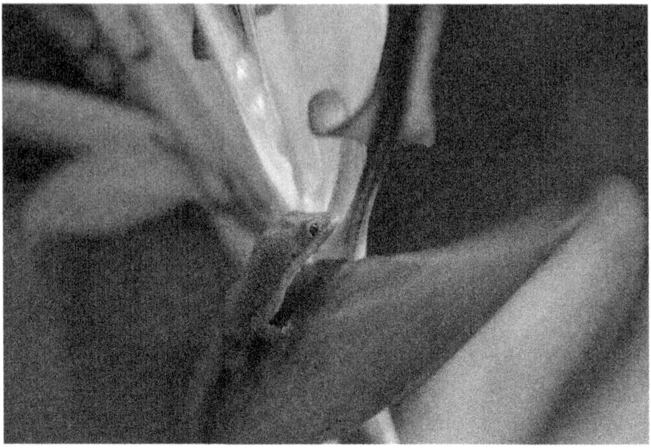

© *Heather 1063*

Furthermore, you can offer the gecko something sweet in the form of a fruit from time to time. Whether the gecko accepts the fruit or not depends on both the species and the character of the animal. Leopard geckos rarely get hold of fruit in the wild and accordingly do not eat it - or at least rarely. Therefore, leopard geckos can do without fruit. Crested geckos and day geckos are more interested in fruit, although their diet is also largely based on insects.

Fruits can be offered either mashed or unpureed. In any case, they should be fully ripened. Different types of berries go down very well with most fruit-eating geckos; they are small and easy to eat. Grapes are also good because of their size and high water content.

In addition, bananas, mangoes, plums, apricots or peaches, for example, can also be offered. However, these types of fruit should always be cut into small, bite-sized pieces beforehand. It is even better if these fruits are pureed beforehand, as this prevents the gecko from choking.

Harder types of fruit such as apples should only be offered pureed. Citrus fruits such as mandarins, lemons or oranges should be avoided altogether, as they are too acidic. But how often should geckos be fed? There is no fixed rule for this. Usually, geckos are fed about three times a week. Each gecko should be fed about four to five insects per feeding.

This is different for young animals - they need to be fed daily at first. Geckos should be fed every day until they are about five to six months old.

But regardless of whether it is a young animal or an adult: a gecko should only be fed bite-sized food, i.e., food that fits comfortably into its small or large mouth. The food should therefore not be wider than the gecko's head! Geckos do not chew their food but swallow it whole.

Whether the insects are placed in the terrarium with tweezers or offered in a food bowl is an individual decision. In any case, a gecko should not be disturbed and stressed too often by humans.

If fruit is offered as well, it should be given no more than twice a week. Especially very sugary fruits like bananas should be used very sparingly. If a gecko generally tends to gain weight, fruit should ideally be offered only once a week or less.

Nocturnal geckos are ideally fed in the evening hours. If this is not possible, they can also be fed during the day. They will then either eat later or interrupt their sleeping phase to feed and continue sleeping afterwards. However, it is better not to interrupt the sleep and offer the food when the gecko has woken up.

One could get the idea of looking for insects for the geckos in the wild. However, whether this is advisable is highly controversial. On the one hand, geckos do not eat as much and not as often - so it actually makes little or no difference to the wallet whether you collect food for the geckos in the wild or not. The financial aspects are negligible, also because many insect species can be grown / bred quite easily at home. This minimises the risk of pathogens or harmful substances.

In addition, collected food from nature offers no added value compared to purchased or home-grown fresh food. The critters from the wild are no better or more nutritious than the purchased food, as long as they are alive or fresh.

Personally, I see no advantage in collecting insects and other foods from the wild. However, I do see some disadvantages and dangers.

Live food can introduce parasites and other pathogens into the gecko's terrarium. With an omnivorous or carnivorous animal like the gecko, the risk of this is always higher than with a herbivorous animal like guinea pigs or rabbits because parasites often use worms and insects as intermediate hosts on which they nest for a while.

If food containing pathogens is introduced into the terrarium, these pathogens and parasites will pass on to the geckos quite quickly and use them as hosts.

Of course, this is also possible if the food is bought or home-bred. As a rule, such a risk cannot be ruled out. However, the risk is higher if the food is collected in the wild.

Other toxins could also be accidentally introduced into the terrarium if the food is obtained from the wild. Here, of course, it depends in which areas and on which land is collected. Pesticides, rat poisons and other harmful substances pose a real risk, which can be avoided if the food is bought fresh or even home-grown.

Of course, geckos also need to drink enough - water is the be-all and end-all for a healthy animal. Therefore, geckos should always have water available so that they can drink at any time of the day or night when they feel thirsty.

Some gecko keepers install a small waterfall in the terrarium. Whether this is useful is also quite controversial because germs can form quite easily and quickly, and pathogens can multiply. Therefore, in many cases a waterfall is not installed.

Often the terrarium is sprayed with water several times a week so that the gecko can lick it off. This kind of water intake is quite popular with geckos. Furthermore, geckos should be provided with a water bowl that is filled with fresh water daily. However, whether the particular gecko will accept a water bowl varies from gecko to gecko - some geckos do not like to drink from a bowl.

If you have such a specimen at home, the terrarium should be sprayed with water even more often. Even if your own gecko is not a big fan of drinking from water bowls, they should still be filled with fresh water at all times in the terrarium to ensure that there is always enough water available. The water bowl should be cleaned regularly, but without chemical cleaning agents. Simple vinegar has an antibacterial effect and is wonderfully suitable for cleaning.

© Torsten Simon

The gecko's tail serves as a fat store, nutrient store and energy store for times of hunger, such as during brumation or when food is scarce. The filled stores in its tail allow the gecko to survive for several weeks without eating. Therefore, the thickness of the gecko's tail indicates how well or poorly the animal has been fed. If the tail is very thin, the gecko should be fed more. If it is too big, the gecko should be "put on a diet" or given food with fewer calories.

By the way: The gecko is capable of shedding its tail. This usually happens in stressful situations, for example when the gecko wants to escape from an enemy quickly. If the gecko lives in a terrarium, it is very rare for the tail to be shed, as the animal is naturally not exposed to enemies at home. However, one should be careful not to disturb, stress or frighten the gecko too often, as this could cause the tail to be shed. Although this will grow back after a while, it should be avoided.

Supplements

Geckos living in a terrarium run the risk of suffering from nutrient deficiencies. Therefore, most breeders and keepers supplement various minerals and vitamins to provide the gecko with everything it needs for a healthy life.

But why is that the case? In the wild, geckos not only eat insects and/or fruits, but they also ingest, for example, specially selected small stones that meet their mineral requirements. Furthermore, animals in the wild get enough vitamin D3 - which is strictly speaking a hormone but is called a vitamin - through direct sunlight on the body. This is not the case in the terrarium if, for example, no special UVA/UVB fluorescent tubes are used. Terrarium sand, tiled floors and the like also do not offer any added value for the coverage of the necessary minerals.

Furthermore, the nutrient supply also depends on what the insects are fed with, which the geckos then eat. If the insects are fed a very one-sided and poor diet, they will naturally not contain all the important nutrients that they could ultimately pass on to the geckos. If you do not breed the insects yourself, it is quite difficult to check how nutritious the purchased insect actually is.

Calcium is an extremely important mineral for geckos and almost always needs to be supplemented. Failure to do so could result in calcium deficiency (hypocalcaemia) or the animals could develop rickets (bone disease; soft and/or bent bones).

Since calcium is so important for the bones, among other things for their construction and stability, calcium should always be freely available to the geckos. Often, a small bowl of calcium powder is permanently offered to the animals in the terrarium. Especially young animals and pregnant females need this for a healthy growth, but adult geckos are also strongly dependent on a sufficient calcium supply. The majority of gecko breeders and keepers resort to cuttlebone powder (or ground cuttlebone shells) for calcium supply. This comes from the cuttlefish and in most cases smells accordingly strong. Therefore, it must be mentioned that not all geckos like cuttlefish powder and consume it. Sometimes the grated cuttlebone is not offered in a small bowl but scattered directly in the terrarium. In pet shops it can often be found with the food for birds. If a gecko does not accept the cuttlebone powder, there are many other odourless calcium powders on the market.

The calcium powder should be offered in a cooler corner of the terrarium and ideally not near the drinking water. It should also be checked regularly to see if the calcium powder has already been used up and/or if there are droppings in the dish.

Calcium powders are divided into calcium citrate and calcium carbonate. Calcium citrate is artificially produced, whereas calcium carbonate is obtained from a naturally occurring source. Therefore, calcium carbonate usually has about four to five times the amount of calcium citrate.

In addition, geckos have an increased vitamin D3 requirement when they are not exposed to UVA/UVB radiation. Vitamin D3 is important for the health of all living creatures. In addition, the supplemented calcium cannot be permanently stored in the bones if there is a vitamin D3 deficiency. For this reason, a vitamin powder should be supplemented that also contains vitamin D3. This vitamin powder can, for example, be sprinkled over the insects to be fed before feeding. It is usually sufficient if the vitamin powder is given at every second or third feeding.

But magnesium and vitamin K are also important for the correct utilisation of vitamin D3 and calcium. Therefore, magnesium and vitamin K should also be found in the vitamin powder.

© *Jill Heyer*

Brumation

Most gecko species hold a brumation. Leopard geckos, crested geckos and day geckos, for example, benefit greatly from brumation and usually hold it in the wild. The tokay gecko does not always hold a brumation in the wild – but it can.

Brumation should be distinguished from hibernation. Some mammals keep a strict hibernation, during which they actually sleep deeply and shut down completely in the long run. Brumation differs from this because the gecko does not sleep completely and continuously, but instead shows a very reduced activity - it just comes to rest for a while. This is not a cold torpor, as is often the case with snakes or amphibians.

During brumation, the gecko's metabolism slows down and its heart beats more slowly. However, geckos are not completely motionless during brumation, but move from time to time, for example to drink.

So why is there a brumation? Brumation is very beneficial to the health of the gecko and usually life is prolonged by taking a brumation. The body has time to regenerate and recover.

Some species, for example the leopard gecko, initiate brumation on their own when the light conditions get darker, and the temperature gets cooler. Slowly they eat less, become quieter and are generally less active. Brumation begins when the days become shorter, the temperatures decrease, and it slowly gets darker. Usually, brumation is initiated in October or November.

Leopard gecko – © Vanessa Peeters

However, it is important that only healthy geckos are "sent" into brumation. Sick animals should not be kept in brumation. Sometimes diseases cannot be detected immediately, so the gecko should be checked for general health and parasites before starting brumation. At the very least, a faecal sample should be submitted to a laboratory for this purpose. If parasites are found, the animal should not go into brumation, as this can cause the parasites to multiply even more and radically worsen the situation.

Animals that should not go into brumation include geckos that have just shed their tails and are currently growing a regenerate tail. For the tail to regrow, the body needs a lot of energy, and the tail also stores the fat and nutrient reserves needed for brumation. If the tail was recently shed, the gecko does not currently have the necessary reserves.

At the beginning of the brumation, the feeding of the gecko is stopped. This is best done at some point between the beginning of October and the beginning of November. The gecko then excretes the food remains that are still in its body. This is important because otherwise the food in the abdomen could start to rot while the gecko is in brumation.

About two weeks after the last feeding, start reducing the lighting time. It is advisable to first reduce the lighting time from twelve to ten hours. Then reduce the lighting time by two hours every week - to eight hours, to six hours, to four hours, to two hours.

Once this point has been reached, all light and heat sources can be switched off.

Whether the gecko then spends the brumation in the terrarium or in a quarantine box is an individual decision. This also depends on where in the house or flat the terrarium is located. If the room is too warm and/or too bright, the gecko should definitely be moved to a cool and dark place during the brumation. Temperatures should be between 10°C and 15°C. These values should neither be exceeded nor fallen short of, so that the metabolism is not abandoned for the brumation mode. A cellar is usually wonderfully suitable for this.

As the gecko only rests and does not sleep all the time, it still needs drinking water and a place to hide. The drinking water should continue to be changed daily, but apart from the necessary water change, the animal should not be disturbed in its rest.

Brumation now lasts about three months. As a rule, the animals do not lose any (or hardly any) weight during this time. However, if they visibly lose weight, the brumation should be stopped.

After brumation, it is important that the gecko is only slowly re-acclimatised to warmer temperatures and more light. The steps that were taken to bring the gecko into brumation are now repeated in reverse order. The lighting time is slowly increased, and the temperatures slowly become warmer. Only when normal conditions are reached again, the gecko is fed again. This is usually the case in March. Before the first feeding, the gecko should have been living under "normal" conditions again for about fourteen days - i.e., a lighting duration of twelve hours and normal temperatures.

Common Diseases

Everyone gets sick once in a while. Some more, others less. Even reptiles like geckos are not immune to diseases, and the severity ranges from "very mild" to "potentially fatal". But how often and how severely a gecko falls ill can be determined to a large extent. As with humans, prevention is the be-all and end-all - a gecko that is kept in a species-appropriate manner, whose needs are met and which receives a balanced and healthy diet, will very rarely become ill. Of course, certain diseases can occur even if a gecko is kept under perfect conditions, for example through heredity or just plain bad luck. However, over 90% of diseases in reptiles are caused by humans - not intentionally, but mostly through simple ignorance of the optimal husbandry conditions.

The most common mistakes with regard to keeping and feeding include, for example ...

... too much dryness in the terrarium (e.g., no wet boxes available)

... overfeeding (leads to overweight, possibly to organ fatty degeneration, etc.)

... no brumation

... stress (e.g., due to lack of space and/or wrong group constellations; e.g., one stressed female on two males etc.)

... fear (e.g., due to too few hiding places)

... too high or too low temperatures

It is not always necessary to visit the vet for every little thing. A visit to the vet is always associated with stress because the gecko is torn away from its familiar environment and has to face a situation that is very stressful and strenuous for it, which, including travel, can sometimes even take several hours.

Nevertheless, for liability reasons, I will not recommend self-treatment and self-medication. Especially beginners may misjudge and treat diseases incorrectly, as they do not have much experience with geckos. I therefore point out that diseases must always be identified and professionally treated by a competent veterinarian.

When choosing a vet, make sure that the person chosen has experience with reptiles. This is an absolute must. Reptiles are so fundamentally different from other pets such as rodents, dogs, cats, etc. that a reptile cannot be treated by just any veterinarian.

A reputable vet will only treat a gecko anyway if they feel confident to do so based on their experience and can treat the animal professionally.

In some areas it can be quite difficult to find a vet who is well versed in reptiles. This varies from region to region. It is possible that a fairly long journey will have to be accepted. A long journey is of course more stressful for the animal, but it is better than having the animal treated by a vet who does not know reptiles well and may make mistakes. Therefore, it is a good idea to start looking for a suitable vet at an early stage in order to have the right contact person at hand immediately in case of an emergency.

Of course, the owner must be sensitised to recognise diseases. If you know your animals, you will notice it quite quickly if something is wrong and if an animal changes. Not every small change has to be a sign of a disease, but the following signs often indicate diseases - especially if they occur in a combination ...

... loss of appetite, refusal of food

... sudden aggressiveness and irritability

... unnatural movements

... changes in the shape, colour and/or consistency of the faeces

... increased need for warm places

... loss of desire to move

... discolouration or fading of the skin

Although a disease is a case for the vet, the owner should be able to recognise the different diseases in principle. Therefore, we will now take a closer look at some common gecko diseases!

1. Abscesses

Abscesses are accumulations of pus that are caused by bacteria. In principle, an abscess can occur in any part of the body. Usually, an abscess is caused by an external injury, for example, a cut on a sharp object. Bacteria can now enter the animal's body through the open wound and possibly cause an infectious abscess.

When reptiles get an abscess, however, the pus inside is usually not liquid, but encapsulated and quite hard. In the worst case, the bursting of the abscess can lead to blood poisoning if the germs enter the bloodstream through it, and the animal can even die. Therefore, many abscesses have to be removed surgically. Whether an operation is necessary and which treatment is appropriate will be decided by the expert veterinarian.

2. Intestinal parasites

Parasites are basically divided into ectoparasites and endoparasites. Ectoparasites are "external living" parasites, for example mites on the skin. Endoparasites are "inside-living" parasites. Intestinal parasites are therefore classified as endoparasites. They include tapeworms, coccidia, hexamites and the like. Almost all animals are infested by parasites sooner or later and this is usually easily treatable.

However, artificially created habitats - for example, in terrariums - will increase infestations quite quickly if they are not recognised and treated early, because there is not much space available in the terrarium. How strong or weak the parasite infestation is often also strongly depends on the animal's psyche. Stress, fear and other negative emotions weaken the animal's immune system and thus its defences.

If an animal is infested with intestinal parasites, this can usually be recognised quite easily from the faeces. The consistency of the faeces becomes soft and resembles mush, and in acute infestation there is often severe diarrhoea.

Sometimes even worms can be seen on the faeces; however, this is not always the case. In addition, the diseased animal often loses weight (sometimes rapidly), even with good nutrition.

3. Diarrhoea

As we noted earlier, intestinal parasites can cause diarrhoea. However, diarrhoea is not always due to a parasite infestation. There are many possible causes of diarrhoea. Since diarrhoea can sometimes dehydrate an animal very quickly, it is important to identify the cause of the faecal change. The dehydration of the body also affects the kidney function, causes a loss of electrolytes and can lead to further intestinal diseases. Diarrhoea is defined not only as watery faeces, but also as mucousy and very soft faeces. There is a particularly urgent need for action if there is even pus and/or blood in the faeces. A specialist veterinarian must be consulted immediately.

Besides intestinal parasites, the following factors can also cause diarrhoea ...

... a lot of stress and other psychological strain

... spoiled food

... feed that is too cold

... too much fruit (too much sugar)

... changing the food too quickly

... overfeeding or malnutrition

... medication

... diseases of the liver or gall bladder

... toxins

© *Regalia Toy*

4. Moulting problems

As reptiles grow throughout their lives, they moult regularly. Many geckos become somewhat dull or whitish shortly before moulting, so that the owner can often easily recognise when a moult is imminent. A healthy gecko which is living under species-appropriate conditions has no problems with moulting and does it without complications. However, if a gecko has moulting problems, the moult will either fail completely or certain parts of the skin will not detach from the gecko's body. In the worst case scenario, moulting problems can cause smaller parts of the body to become strangulated, as they can no longer be well supplied with blood - this mainly affects the tip of the tail and the toes. In most cases, moulting problems are due to insufficient humidity in the terrarium. Conditions that are too dry sometimes make moulting immensely difficult. In addition, geckos often support their moult by rubbing the "old" skin on objects such as stones. If the gecko has no possibility to rub off the skin, problems often occur as well. Other diseases such as dehydration or infections can also make moulting difficult, but too dry conditions and lack of opportunities to rub off the skin are the two most common causes of problems. Particularly in the winter months, the air humidity sometimes drops extremely, so it is important to ensure that the air humidity is sufficiently high, especially in the colder months.

5. Heat stroke

Especially in summer, you should make sure that it does not get too hot in the terrarium. Depending on the terrarium, heat can sometimes build up, especially if the terrarium is too small and/or does not have enough ventilation. Therefore, you should keep a close eye on the temperatures during the hot months. Even if heating mats or similar devices are used, overheating can sometimes occur. It is also particularly risky if the terrarium is exposed to direct sunlight - then the temperature can rise extremely within a very short time. If it is too hot, there is a risk of heat stroke. In the worst case scenario, this can even lead to death. The animals often become lethargic and restless, sometimes they even suffer locomotor disorders or foam at the mouth. They try to cool down, but this is often not possible within the confines of the terrarium. If an animal suffers a heat stroke, it should be taken out of the terrarium immediately and moved to a cooler place.

The animal should be stabilised by a cool bath or cool wet cloths. However, make sure that the water is not too cold! You want to stabilise the temperature quickly but cooling too brutally can cause a shock! In addition, the animal must now drink a lot of water. However, a gecko should not suffer from heat stroke in the first place.

6. Liver diseases

Liver diseases occur quite frequently in reptiles when the liver is permanently overloaded due to incorrect housing conditions. The liver is a detoxification organ and also needs a break now and then. An unhealthy lifestyle puts too much strain on the liver, and it cannot recover from its work.

Therefore, liver diseases are usually caused when an animal is fed too often on a permanent basis and/or is given food that is too high in calories. People sometimes "mean too well" for the animal and overfeed it.

However, this is detrimental to their health, as geckos simply have a different nutritional rhythm than, for example, humans or other popular pets. A lack of brumation can also lead to liver diseases or diseases of other organs, as the body has plenty of time to recover and regenerate during brumation.

Liver diseases develop rather slowly, so that at first there are usually no symptoms. At a later stage, the urine and faeces of the diseased animal often become discoloured and take on an unnatural colour.

7. Egg binding

When females have problems laying eggs, this is called “egg binding”. The eggs may either not be laid at all or only partially, they may block the cloaca and/or the fallopian tube, cause a prolapse and, in the worst case scenario, may even rot in the animal's body. In acute egg binding that is not treated in time, the animal may even die - for example, from blood poisoning or kidney failure. The blockages can lead to bloated bellies, cramps, food refusal and the like. Egg binding can occur, for example, when a female is not encouraged by a male to lay eggs. But egg binding can also occur if there are no suitable places to lay eggs. In addition, deficiency symptoms such as vitamin D deficiency are often a reason for egg binding. In order to prevent egg binding, a sufficient supply of all necessary vitamins and minerals should be ensured. Egg-laying sites should also not be lacking. If egg binding still occurs, a veterinarian with experience in reptiles should be consulted as soon as possible.

8. Mouth rot (stomatitis)

Stomatitis is an infection in the mouth of the animal. In geckos, however, stomatitis usually occurs less frequently than in other reptiles, such as turtles or snakes. Stomatitis often develops as a result of other infections in the body or parasite infestations. General metabolic disorders can also trigger the disease. If the oral mucosa is injured, stomatitis has an easy time. If there is also a wound in the mouth, this can also lead to a bacterial infection. In the worst case scenario, stomatitis can even cause blood poisoning and abscesses can form. The sick animal often dehydrates quite quickly and often refuses food.

9. Mites

Mites are parasites that - unlike worms, for example - do not live inside the animal but on the skin. Therefore, they are often visible from the outside, but this is not always the case. The more severe the infestation, the more likely it is that even a layperson can recognise a mite infestation. Mites like to nest in "corners", so they mainly infest the cloaca, the corners of the mouth, the ears, the bends of the joints and similar parts of the body. Mites cause itching, so affected geckos usually rub themselves on objects to relieve the itch. The stronger the immune system, the better the animals cope with mites. If the immune system is not particularly good anyway, for example due to an unhealthy diet or stress, the animal suffers particularly badly from the infestation. As a rule, a mite infestation must be treated with appropriate medication, which the expert veterinarian will prescribe. It is also important to clean the terrarium thoroughly and replace the substrate to avoid a new infestation after treatment.

10. Kidney diseases

Kidney diseases - similar to liver diseases - are quite common in reptiles. Similar to the liver, the kidneys also take care of detoxifying the body. The kidneys function like a toxin filter for the body and they remove germs and other pathogens from the body. If the kidneys are diseased, the urine is usually discoloured, too dark, somewhat slimy or too cloudy. Like liver disease, kidney disease develops rather slowly and insidiously, but it is almost always triggered by incorrect husbandry conditions. For healthy kidneys, sufficient fluid intake is the be-all and end-all. Therefore, it is essential that the animals always have enough fresh water available. If an animal is dehydrated or does not drink enough water, this can lead to severe damage to the kidneys in the long run. But hypothermia can also lead to kidney damage over time. Therefore, always make sure that the temperature zones are appropriate.

11. Rickets

Rickets is also often called metabolic bone disease. It is a disease of the bones caused by a permanent calcium deficiency. A calcium deficiency is also called hypocalcaemia. Sufficient calcium intake - in combination with vitamins D and K and magnesium - is essential and absolutely necessary for a healthy and stable skeleton. In rickets, there is reduced bone density and a change in bone composition. Especially young animals and pregnant females have an increased need for the aforementioned micronutrients. Unfortunately, rickets is relatively common in geckos, so prevention is very important. Damage is usually very difficult or impossible to cure. If an animal has rickets, the bones become soft, and they deform. In very bad cases, the gecko may only be able to move by crawling on its belly. Deformities can occur and the bones can thicken in certain places. Rickets can cause secondary diseases, as the affected animal often has restricted mobility, suffers from calcification and kidney diseases, has problems eating due to deformed jaws and much more. Egg binding can also occur in females. It is therefore essential that rickets does not occur in the first place - through sufficient supply of the essential micronutrients.

12. Tail shedding

In the wild, many geckos throw off their tails when they are in an acutely dangerous situation and are threatened by an enemy. By dropping the tail, the enemy is distracted and, in all likelihood, concentrates on the tail that has just been dropped, which continues to "wriggle" for a while. The gecko can thus get to safety. In the terrarium at home, it does not often happen that a gecko drops its tail, because it is not exposed to natural enemies. In rare cases, however, it still happens that an animal throws off its tail. Usually, acute stress or acute fear is the trigger. In itself, it is not dangerous when a gecko gets rid of its tail. It grows back slowly, but not like the "original" tail. The gecko does not suffer from this, it is rather a blemish. Nevertheless, a tail shedding is suboptimal, because the gecko stores its nutrients in its tail for bad times or for winter months. Therefore, geckos with a shed tail should not be put into brumation, as they simply cannot fall back on the necessary reserves. In the case of the affected gecko, special attention should be paid to the food supply so that the gecko can replenish its energy reserves and access all the necessary micro- and macronutrients it needs to regrow its tail. It will probably grow back thicker and shorter than the original tail. However, there is usually no need to worry about the "wound" as the blood vessels will automatically close and there will be little or no bleeding when the tail is shed. Nevertheless, one should keep an eye on the development of the wound and consult the vet in case of inflammation or similar complications.

13. Excess weight

If a gecko suffers from excess weight, this is almost always due to poor husbandry. As a rule, this is simply because the animal is fed too often and/or too much energy. In the wild, you will hardly find an overweight animal, as the animals there take care of finding food themselves, generally move more and regulate their food intake better themselves. All this is omitted when keeping animals at home and the human is responsible for selecting and regulating the food for the animal. Excess weight can - as in humans - cause many other diseases and is often the reason for fatty liver, kidney diseases, rickets, etc.

© *Anrita*

Legal Notice

Author: Alina Daria Djavidrad

Contact: Wahlerstraße 1, 40472 Düsseldorf, Germany

1st edition (2021)

© M. Laranda

© *Cubialpha*

Room for Notes

Printed in Great Britain
by Amazon

73200772R00066